Ruby
in the
Middle

Written by Sarah O'Neil

Illustrated by Omar Aranda

Flying Start
to Literacy®

Contents

Chapter 1:

When the wind came up

Ruby was out on the lake, looking for food. There was no wind and the water was flat. It was easy for Ruby to find lots of food. She put her head under the water and began to eat.

But then the wind began to blow
and there were waves on the water.
Ruby couldn't put her head
under the water to find food.

"Hurry," said the wise flamingo. "If we stand together, we can stop the waves. Then we will be able to find food."

Ruby swam very fast. She went right to the middle of the flock. This was the best place to find food, because there were no waves.

Chapter 2:

Staying in the middle

At first, the other flamingos didn't mind Ruby being in the middle of the flock.

They always took turns at being in the middle and being on the edge. This was how they looked for food when the wind blew and there were waves on the lake.

"It's Ruby's turn to be in the middle," they said.

But then it was Ruby's turn to be on
the edge of the flock.

"I'm not moving," said Ruby, and
she stuck her head under the water.

"But you have to move. It's your turn!"
said the other flamingos.
"Everyone has a turn on the edge
and then everyone has a turn in
the middle."

Chapter 3:

Moving on

There was one flamingo who could see what Ruby was doing. It was the wise flamingo.

"It is time for Ruby to learn how to be part of our flock," she said.

The wise flamingo whispered to the other flamingos. Slowly, the flamingos began to move down the lake and away from Ruby.

Soon Ruby was standing all alone.
At first, she didn't notice.

But then a wave slapped her in the
face. The wind ruffled her feathers.

There were too many waves for her
to find food.

"I must get back to the flock,"
said Ruby. "I must get back
in the middle where
I belong."

Ruby flew over the flock and tried to land in the middle.

"Let me in! Let me in!" she called.

But the flamingos would not let Ruby in.

"If you will not take your turn on the edge like the rest of us," said the flamingos, "you cannot be part of the flock."

Chapter 4:

All alone

Ruby landed on the edge of the lake. She was all by herself. The wise flamingo came up to Ruby.

"I cannot feed without the rest of the flock," said Ruby.

"That is true," said the wise flamingo.

"And the flock will not let me feed with them," said Ruby.

"That is also true," said the wise flamingo.

"It's not fair!" said Ruby.

"Were you being fair when you stayed in the middle of the flock all the time?" said the wise flamingo.

Ruby hung her head in shame.

The wise flamingo was right. Ruby didn't deserve a place in the flock.

"What can I do?" said Ruby.

"You must show the flock that you have changed," said the wise flamingo.

From that day on, when the wind blows and there are waves on the lake, Ruby always takes her place on the edge of the flock. And she happily waits for her turn in the middle.

Ruby is part of the flock again.

A note from the author

I was amazed when I found out that when the wind blows and there are waves on the lakes where flamingos live, they can't put their heads under the water to feed. But if they stand together in a huge group, the water in the middle of the flock is much flatter and here they can feed.

It made me wonder how flamingos have learned to do this. What would happen if one bird was stubborn and refused to move from the middle? And that is how the idea for Ruby was born.